The Makings of a Wonderer

Angela Pinkall

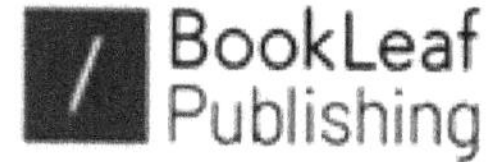

BookLeaf Publishing

Presentation by *BookLeaf Publishing*

Web: www.bookleafpub.com

E-mail: info@bookleafpub.com

ISBN: 9789357211017

First edition 2022

DEDICATION

To my fellow wonderers

ACKNOWLEDGEMENT

I'm so grateful first and foremost to God for the gift of creativity and writing.

Thank you to my husband as well, for encouraging me to pursue my passions, no matter how big or small.

And thank you to anyone and everyone who will read even one of these poems.

Wonder

Lying here in bed,
in wonder of breath.
Can't help but watch my chest
rise and fall and rise and fall again.

This tiny organ—
as small as my fist—
functions to keep me alive and to thrive.

It makes no sense.
A perfect mess,
I am a body of cells, I confess.

Stringed together
with imperfect thoughts
and illogical ways,
a mess of emotions lost in a haze.

And yet I breathe—
I inhale air.
I am alive,
so there's purpose there.

And emotions mix with this body of cells!
There's so much more in me that dwells
and comes alive at my Maker's touch.

This truth astounds me—it's almost too much—
that'd I'd be his for a purpose, a reason.

So it's in him I believe in
and worship and honor and live for each season.
Each day of my life,
I devote to Christ,
who calls me his own,
who never leaves me to flounder alone,
but who lifts me up.

He fills my cup,
and he lifts my head
and called me to life from the dead.

So I thank him for his kindness,
his mercy,
his grace,
his truth.
I thank him for making everything brand new.
I thank him for changing me from the inside out.
From these hills, I'll praise his name with a
shout.

And may it be known that forever I'm his.
When all is lost I'll cling to this—
the fact Christ loves me
and chose me
and burst through hell's gate to hold me!

What more could I want?
If the world knew this—if only.
But we're here to tell them,
as I'm here to tell you:
that Christ isn't just for me.
He longs for you, too,
to make you brand new,
so you could do things you never dreamed of
and never knew,
so you could be set ablaze with his holy fire,
and live the life that Christ desires.

So pour out your life a broken surrender,
and watch him reignite those dying embers.
Come alive with the wonder of life—
no more hopelessness or strife.
Only grace and truth abide,
no room for condemnation to hide.
Cast aside the broken promises and lies
and find in Christ all that satisfies.

Journey

Life is like a journey,
and it's one that all must take.
Some paths we tread are simple,
while others end in heartbreak.

We strive to go the distance
and complete the trip begun,
but the journey never ceases,
no matter the miles run.

Life is like a journey
or a road trip we all start.
We all start with life's first breath
and then end at different parts.

Life is like a journey;
at some point, it will end.
But when we think it's over,
it's only an unforeseen bend.

Two chairs

Where there is now one chair,
soon there will be two.
This one's for me;
the other will be for you.

This is where I sat and waited,
cried and pleaded,
pounding the seat in all my frustration—
lonely and broken in my desperation.

This is where I sat and waited,
whole and content,
no longer walking around in brokenness—
You called my heart from its hopelessness.

Redeemed and restored!
Because our love? It's worth fighting for,
praying for,
waiting for,
believing for!
I keep knocking on heaven's door,
that I will find the one my soul longs for.

And You, the picture of love and grace,
is evident with every smile on his face.

And I know that I know
that You did this to show
Your power,
Your glory,
Your splendor,
Your might!
That you were there for me during the darkest
night
when I felt rejected, neglected,
unworthy, unloved—
You came for me with the fiercest of loves.

Calling my name:
Daughter, beloved,
Your time will come.
But dance in My presence,
until I unveil your prince.

Where there was once one chair,
now there is be two.
This one's for me;
The other one is for you.

This is where we sip our coffee,
talk and relax,
discussing our plans and what to do today,
content and together because God paved the
way.

This is where we have our breakfast,
or just catch up.
No longer walking around in loneliness—
God brought us together despite our mess.

Sunday sleep

I went to bed Sunday,
thinking, hoping, knowing that
this week needs to be different.

This week is a new week,
please, it simply has to be
because all my energy is spent.

Weeks of Sunday scaries,
dreading the week to come,
doing all of this again.

I went to bed Sunday,
with a glimmer of some hope,
something new would soon begin.

I see it so clearly
and not quite clearly at all.
But it is a new day now!

A new wind is blowing,
the winds of change are coming
from somewhere, really, somehow.

When I sleep next Sunday,

hope will arrest me once more:
I will have purpose restored.

I'll wake up, heart on fire,
excited for all to come—
Joy at work is my reward!

Wild

Distracted, you're walking blind.
Two steps ahead, now five behind.
Looking for answers that you can't find—
how much more meaning you'd see in life,
If you chose God each and every time!
Looking for escape instead of what's real,
you put bandaids over wounds that only He can
heal.
You search for acceptance in anyone's eyes
and close your heart and believe the lies,
feasting on scraps and not His Word.
You settle for less than what you are worth.

I question His goodness and look for something
more,
but that search is in vain—
these longings are what He came for:
to put pain in its place,
to usher in grace,
to give us permission to look at His face,
and find the answers we're too scared to even
ask,
to let us be real and remove the mask.

In the chaos, I heard him say,
"Daughter, beloved, look my way.
You spend time on anything and everything but
me,
yet I'm the only one who sets your heart free.
You choose anyone and everyone who isn't me,
looking for security in their company.
Yet your identity is anchored in me.
Listen to this conversation that I'm trying to
have:
I want your whole heart, yet you give me only
half—
and sometimes not even that.

"You give me pieces when it fits your
preconceived notion
of what a perfect life should be.
You go through each religious motion,
searching for life apart from me,
as you turn to other idols that you pray will
satisfy,
forgetting and neglecting the one who died to
give you life."

Hope answers with a call to salvation.
He's crying for my love and all my adoration.
Yet I walk past him as I do each day,
lost in the moment lost in my own way,
lost in my dreams and caught in fantasies.

He's called me to a purpose greater than these.
And yet He calls—
His voice can't be kept out of the walls
I built around my heart.
His voice breaks those walls apart:
a quiet whisper,
a desperate plea,
a loud shout of victory!
Gently, firmly, louder still—
My love echoes eternal valleys to hills.
And when my love for you could grow no more,
I tucked it in a baby for all to adore.

But I loved you too much to leave love
infant-sized.
Love was nailed to a cross,
so death met its demise.
And now your choice is between life and death:
the ways of this world
or the wonder of my breath.
So put aside business and trivial distraction—
come alive in me and for me:
I've called your heart to action.
No longer walking distracted!
But on fire with life and passion!
It's gonna be better than your craziest dreams—
the best is yet to come despite how it seems.
Walk as my daughter, my child.
Hold my hang 'cause it's gonna be wild.

A love like that

When she asked you what love was,
you said you saw it in me—
in the love I shared with your grandma
and in our chemistry.

You know, we worked for this love—
it was far from a stroll in the park.
How we loved in the day,
we chose to maintain in the dark.

To have, to hold, to cherish—
such simple words, or so they seem.
To choose, to trust, to protect—
this love might be harder than you'd dream.

But is it worth it, you wonder.
Oh yes, without a doubt.
Two lives joined, united together—
That's what marriage is about.

Fight for a love like that.
It's the best, I promise you.
Love in word, action, and thought—
and in everything else you do.

Skippy

Cold nose
Warm heart
Four paws in each direction sprawled,
gnawing on your favorite tennis ball.
You all but destroyed the house that one day
when we had that summer storm in May.
But I forgave you
because how could I not?
From the very start,
you had your paws wrapped around my heart.
And your happy wag is all I know
and has been since I brought you home so long
ago.
Now I call you my old man, my Skippy Poo.
I hope you know how much I love you.
But it's not all roses and butterflies
because when you fart, it smells like something
died!
I glare at you and choke and laugh,
but I'm sure one day I'll want that smell back.
We trudge along on your daily stroll,
since too much exercise takes its toll.
You stop and sniff for nearly an eternity,
and I remember when you used to pull me!
Then you stop to roll in the perfect grassy place

with a pure look of happiness on your face.
Going on fourteen, you're my old man, I know,
and I can't help but wonder where'd the time
go?
So I'll let you use dad's fluffy robe as your bed,
and I'll try not to complain about how much you
shed.
I'll try to go slower on our daily walk
and let you enjoy the smells of the block.
I'll try to give you a few extra treats now and
then
as a too-small thank you for being my friend.
I'll try to give you extra pets each night
and hope it reminds you how you've brought joy
to my life.

Ellie

Tiny legs
Stubby tail
You sploot in your superhero pose,
with each leg stretched out down to your toes.
We thought you'd never be potty trained!
Cleaning up after you was such a pain!
You rarely went for shoes in your quest to
destroy—
instead, you preferred any squeaky toy.
And you were worth it
because it is you.
From the very start,
you had your paws wrapped around my heart.
And I've said that before, sure,
but trust me, it's no less true with you.
I call you my sweet girl, my Ellie Bellie.
You're full of sass and personality.
You put our foster pups at ease;
somehow your playfulness gives them peace.
Your zoomies awe me with your speed,
and on any walk, you always take the lead
until you find something to stop and sniff—
then your legs refuse to budge an inch.
So we give you a pull and call your name,

until, finally, we are back on our way.
Then you stop just to bask in a warm, sunny place
with a pure look of happiness on your face.
Going on just two, you're still a pup, I know,
but I can't help but wish that the time would slow.
So I'll give you extra cuddles before bed,
and I'll try not to complain about how much you shed.
I'll try to get you to the dog park some more
because I know how you love to explore.
I'll try to give you belly rubs now and then
as a token of love for my furry friend.
I'll fill my phone with cute photos of you
and look back one day at just how quickly the time flew.

Lilly

Long legs
Happy tail
You nap in the sunniest spot.
You've earned that nap; you've been through a
lot.
A foster from Puerto Rico,
we had to take everything super slow.
You barely let us touch you when you first came
to stay,
but now all you want to do is to play.
And oh, how we love you,
because how could we not?
From the very start,
you had your paws wrapped around my heart.
Though I say that every time,
Last I checked, loving pups is no crime.
But if it is, dear girl, my Silly Lilly,
you'll find me guilty and so easily.
You really are so truly silly
especially when you climb that tree!
I've never seen a dog do that.
The first time, I almost had a heart attack!
But now I laugh as you explore your world,
and marvel at how far you've come, girl.

When you first came home, we couldn't touch
you.
You were just too scared from all the past abuse.
Now, you practically demand love and affection,
and you moo like a cow to get attention.
Going on two or three, we don't really know,
but you're so loved now, and we won't let you
go—
unless there's a family who deserves you
and will give you the best natural treats to chew.
But for now, you're home and here to stay
because we don't know if you'll leave one day.
So I'll cuddle you as we watch tv
and trust and hope you now feel safe with me.
So rest at ease in your favorite space,
and know that this is your home, and it is a safe
place.

At the beach

Looking at my to-do list—
why is it a mile long?
I want to lose myself at the beach
and listen to nature's song.

The sound of the surf,
and the crash of the waves
leaves my heart in wonder,
and I take it in, amazed.

The sun hot on my face,
the wind whipping my hair—
I dream for a moment,
and wish I was there.

There's something about the water,
something about the beach,
that makes my problems seem smaller
and my worries out of reach.

I close my eyes for a moment,
and I feel gloriously free.
I can almost taste the salt in the air,
and feel the sun beating down on me.

The noise of the world dulls
at the edge of the sea.
There's just water and sky
as far as I can see.

I feel smaller for a moment,
which I don't really mind.
I actually feel alive
and leave troubles behind.

The magic of the ocean
is that it pulls you in.
Not the tide itself,
but the ocean's commotion.

The beach is truly an experience:
sights, tastes, sounds, and smells!
Maybe it's too much for some,
but something in me quiets and quells.

I sit in my chair,
book in my hand.
I breathe it all in
and finally understand.

Come back to peace,
to the sea with its sunsets and tides.
Soak it in and revel in it:
this peace the ocean provides.

A year

It was a good year,
a bad year.
I burst through walls
and conquered fears.
Dreams were made—
and crushed—
in those 365 days.
I saw the moon blacken the sun,
and my muscles burned after every run.
I smiled
and cried
and joked
and laughed.
And while I'm looking ahead,
I still look back.
One eye on the future
and one on the past:
to see where I've come from
and where I'll go yet.
There's beauty there, despite the tears.
the past can't hold a candle to the light of my
future years.

Home

It sure is an adventure
to buy a house together.

You want a huge yard,
and I couldn't care less.
You want some acreage and land,
and as for me? Not even close, I confess.
You want something that reminds you of your
childhood days
and your grandparents and the memories you
made.
I want something that just feels like our own,
unattached to the past and that evolves as we
both grow.
I want aesthetic, you could say I'm pickier.
One closet?! God forbid—I need a his and hers.
Let me look at the kitchen—the cabinets,
counters, and sink.
It all needs an upgrade, don't you think?
Don't get me started on the paint on this wall.
Just looking at the ugly shade makes my skin
crawl.
The yard is simply too big—just imagine the
mess.
I've gone on and on, and so I digress.

It sure is an adventure
to choose a home together.

We can paint this wall—
add a light in that hall.
It really doesn't matter—
I already have my happily ever after.
It's not the size of the lot or even the square
feet—
with you and the dogs, I'm as content as can be.
Together is my favorite place to be—
all that matters about our home is that you're
there with me.
I want a place to make memories with you.
We don't need need a lake to have a fantastic
view.
Although, if I'm being real, a lake-view would
be really nice
(but somewhere warm since I don't do ice).
Who knows where we'll end up five, ten years
from now?
I'm sure it'll blow my mind and I'll just say
wow.
I'll look at you in your rocking chair right by my
side—
and whisper, it's been one hell of a ride.

It sure is an adventure
to build a life together.

Sunset

Magic touched the clouds,
and they glowed.
And once the light was gone,
it wasn't that the magic had gone.
It was that the night brought a spell
all its own.

In the desert

The ragged
   Brick-red buildings
      Stacked upon each other
Their differences marked only
   By the colorful tapestries that were clothing
      Hanging from each balcony
Marking signs of life
The dust blurring the space between sky and
earth
The smell permeating every fiber of clothing and
every pore of our skin

Still

So still,
Still your racing heart next to mine.
Tell me that it's gonna be just fine.

And even,
Even though you might be lyin',
Tell me we're ok we'll just keep on tryin'.

We're dyin',
Dyin' to see what else is there,
Exhausted from breathing without air.

But hope,
Hope as the silence gives way to song,
Fight because you've been made strong.

And live,
Live 'cause the darkness gives way to light,
Live free from the chains that once bound you
tight.

Since now,
Now you're alive, prisoner no more,
Walking in freedom you were made for.

Life

What is this fragile thing called life?
That in an instant it can go out like a light.
In the snap of a finger,
it's just the memories that linger.

And in those moments,
I don't need the messy details,
or else—like a train off its tracks—
every thought derails.

I just need peace,
an hour—maybe two—
of sweet, sweet sleep.

Yet my mind won't rest,
debating between what's good and what's best.

I've been awake for hours,
reliving horrible but precious memories
that were ours.

Horrible because they're gone,
precious because they happened.
No matter what, life just goes on.

So mind does battle in the hours of the night,
fighting between strength
and the fragility of life.

Death

For my grandparents.

Death broke down your door
in the dark hours this morning.
Death stole your last breath
and left us in mourning.
Death laughed in what it thought was its victory.
Oh, but death didn't know its own defeat.

Death didn't know it was already doomed
because in the very moment it broke down your
door,
you were already on streets of gold,
walking,
running with lungs that needed no oxygen mask,
in a body that knew no cancer.

You spun around,
breathing in the freedom
and the joy
and the peace
and the love—
and you let out a giggle you'd only known as a
child.
And you knew you were home.

Hope

Hope met doubt.
Joy met fear
as we bared our souls
in this moment here.

What did we know?
What would we find
racing down this road
leaving logic behind?

Sorrow and longing
love and regret—
time heals those wounds,
but the heart can't forget.

Circles race in my head—
and still do when I think
of what we could be...
I feel my heart sink.

But I have a secret—
I've tied hope to my heart.
It preserves my life
and keeps me afloat in this part.

As if tomorrow never comes

Dance in your underwear,
and scream at the top of your lungs.
Run without looking back,
and love as if tomorrow never comes.

Burst out in song for no reason,
and give your loved ones hugs.
Chase down your wildest dreams,
and live as if tomorrow never comes.

Embrace the seemingly small moments,
as you dance to your own drum.
Live this moment to the fullest,
and laugh as if tomorrow never comes.

So love through the strain,
live through the pain,
and laugh in the rain.
In the end, smile, see how far you've come,
and know you'd do it again
as if tomorrow never comes.

Dreaming

I'm dreaming
of meaning—
of doing something
I actually believe in.
I'm not about the hustle or grind—
I need a different pace to clear my mind.
I don't want another team chat or one-on-one
sync.
I want to catch my breath and just think.
I'm tired of staring at this computer screen
clearing emails that don't apply to me.
Editing this piece or tweaking that word—
the monotony of this is truly absurd.
It's a good job, it's a good job, I repeat.
Just because it's good doesn't mean it's for me.
I also repeat it's not that bad daily.
Has my voice sounded a bit strangled lately?
It wouldn't surprise me if that were so
because this isn't the way I thought life would
go.
I have these questions, day in and day out.
They bubble to the surface until I SHOUT:
Who does this help?
Whose life does it touch?
I just want to make a difference,

or is that asking too much?
I'm tired of the pointless, endless pings.
I want to do something that makes my heart
sing—
something that puts joy in my life
and makes me feel, well, alive—
something that furthers someone else's
aspirations,
or maybe moves them forward in their pursuit of
education—
something meaningful and actually worthwhile,
maybe it would spark a genuine smile.
I guess simply put, I just want it to matter.
Something that makes a difference—
now that's what I'm after.

From wanderer to wonderer
and back again

How does a wanderer come to be?
I'll tell you my story since it happened to me.

A wanderer is simply one who wonders
at the world that they see.
It's that wondering that lights the fire,
now travel is their utmost desire.

To get on a plane or jump in their car,
there's no distance that's too far.
There's also no distance too close—
just a trip downtown can be an adventurous
dose.

To capture memories with film or ink—
that's joy, or that's what I think.
And there is joy in that, to be sure,
but don't miss out on the moment's allure.

In the moment is where a wonderer comes to
life,
as they wonder what it is that makes passions
ignite.
It it art, numbers, words, or medicine?

Is it politics, debates, hopes, or religion?
Is it peace or wartime or excessive ambition?
It's in the details that humanity creeps in.

To wander is incredible, I can attest.
But maybe to wonder is by far the best.
It's the wondering that prompts us to learn more,
which ignites the wanderer's heart to explore.
You see, you can't wander without the wonder,
for it's the wonder that births the urge to wander.

My book is a collection of musings and freeform poetry exploring the idea of what it is to wonder at the world around us—and just the joy and pain that make up the human experience.

About the Author

Angela Pinkall has been in love with writing since she was in fifth grade. She currently writes educational content as her main focus, but she also enjoys writing on her blog whenever inspiration strikes. Along with her husband and their three dogs, Angela lives in sunny Florida but enjoys escaping the state (and the country, for that matter) anytime a travel opportunity comes up. No matter where she goes, she's sure to bring her camera, a pen, and a notebook, so she can articulately capture her incredible experiences (even if she just shares them with her family and friends).

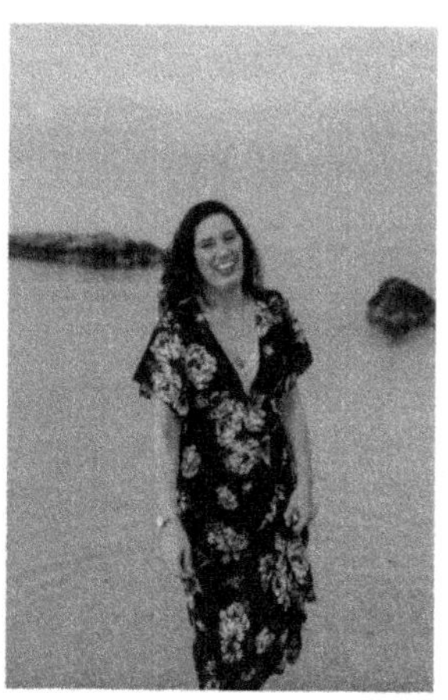

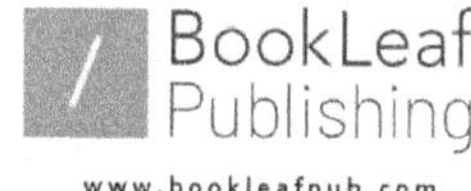

CPSIA information can be obtained
at www.ICGtesting.com
Printed in the USA
LVHW070014140623
749500LV00008B/192